LETTERS TO COLLEGE STUDENTS

LESSONS ON LIFE, FUTURE & BUILDING A SUCCESSFUL CAREER

DR. ASHISH GUPTA

Made with ♥ on the Notion Press Platform
www.notionpress.com

To every college student who's ever felt lost, confused,
underestimated, or unsure of the future—
This book is for you.

Contents

Contents

Copyright

For permissions and inquiries, contact:
Email: authorashishgupta@gmail.com
Website: ashishgupta.co.in

This book is a work of non-fiction. While every effort has been made to ensure accuracy, the author and publisher shall not be held responsible for any errors, omissions, or outcomes related to the application of the ideas presented.

First Edition: 2025

Preface

Dear Friend,

I didn't write this book as a teacher. I wrote it as a friend, a mentor, and someone who has spent the last 14+ years working with students, listening to their dreams, their doubts, and their struggles.

Every year, I meet bright young minds entering college full of hope and potential—but also confusion.

"What should I do with my life?"
"Will I be successful?"
"Am I doing enough?"
"Is this the right path?"

The world today is moving faster than ever, and college students are caught in a constant race—degrees, placements, certifications, competition, expectations. Amid all this noise, what often gets lost is guidance with heart, advice with honesty, and lessons rooted in real life.

That's where this book comes in.

"Letters to College Students" is a sequel to my earlier work, **Letters to Teenagers,** which helped young minds navigate school life with clarity and courage. This time, I wanted to speak to those who are now stepping into adulthood—those navigating the exciting, overwhelming, and transformational phase called college.

But this is not a textbook.
It's not filled with lectures or theories.
It's a collection of 27 personal letters—written like I'm sitting across from you, having a real conversation about career, mindset, skills, failures, friendships, and life.

This book is meant to do three things:

- Help you make sense of your college journey
- Equip you with tools to build a meaningful career
- Remind you that success is not a destination—it's a process of becoming

If you're a college student seeking clarity, motivation, or simply a little guidance in this big, complex world—you'll find a friend in these pages.

You don't need to have it all figured out.
You just need to start—with awareness, intention, and belief.

Let's build something great—together.

With warmth and purpose,
Dr. Ashish Gupta
Life & Career Coach | Mentor | Author

A Letter To My College Friends

Dear Friend,

Welcome to one of the most exciting phases of your life. You're young, full of dreams, and standing at the edge of possibilities.

College is more than just a place to earn a degree—it's the launchpad for the rest of your life. It's where you begin to shape your identity, make meaningful friendships, test your limits, and most importantly, start building your career and character. And trust me, both are equally important.

I've written this book because I know how confusing, overwhelming, and fast-paced these years can feel. One moment you're trying to make sense of who you are, and the next you're expected to have your whole future figured out. That pressure is real. And so is the noise around you—**"Do an MBA," "Start a startup," "Get a government job," "Go abroad"**... Everyone seems to have an opinion about your life.

But here's what I want you to remember:
This is your journey. You get to write your own story.

In my years of working with students, guiding thousands of young minds, and observing career paths unfold in unexpected ways, I've realized one thing—success is not about who's the smartest in the room, but who's the most prepared, most focused, and most consistent.

This book is a collection of letters—just like a friend, mentor, or elder sibling might write. These are not lectures. They're life lessons. Practical, real, and rooted in experience. From finding clarity and beating procrastination to building career capital and dealing with failures, I've put together what I wish someone had told me in my college years.

Whether you're confused about your career path, struggling to stay motivated, or just want to make the most of your college years—this book is for you.

You're not alone in this journey. And you don't need to have it all figured out yet.
But what you do need is the right mindset, the right tools, and the right guidance. That's what I hope this book becomes for you—a trusted companion in your journey of becoming who you were meant to be.

With all my heart,
I believe in you.

Warm regards,
Ashish

Why This Book Matters

Every generation has its own challenges. But your generation—our college students today—are growing up in a world that changes faster than ever before.

New careers are emerging. Old jobs are disappearing. Technology is evolving at lightning speed. And while you're trying to figure out who you are, the world is already asking you, *"What's your plan?"*

That's a lot to take in.

Colleges prepare you with knowledge. But life and career demand much more—**clarity, confidence, decision-making, communication, adaptability, and purpose.** Unfortunately, many students step out of college with a degree in hand, but no direction in mind.

This book is my humble attempt to change that.

It matters because **your career is too important to be left to luck.**
It matters because **you deserve guidance that speaks your language—real, relatable, and relevant.**
It matters because **the right lessons at the right time can shape your entire future.**

This book is not written by a professor in a classroom or a motivational speaker on a stage. It's written by someone who has spent more than a decade working closely with students like you—mentoring, hiring, guiding, and watching what works (and what doesn't).

Whether you're confused about your next step, curious about building a great life, or just want to do more than the bare minimum in college—this book will help you:

- Make sense of the chaos
- Discover your true strengths
- Build habits that lead to success
- Avoid common mistakes
- Learn from real-world experiences
- And most importantly, start taking action

If my book "Letters to Teenagers" was about helping teenagers navigate life with clarity and courage, this one is about **helping college students build careers with confidence and character.**

Because your career is not just about what job you get—it's about the life you build.
And the time to start building that life is **now.**

Let's begin.

From Teenager To Young Adult: What Changes

Growing up is not marked by age. It's marked by awareness.

As a teenager, life often feels like it's about doing what you're told—attending school, preparing for exams, following rules, and trying to fit in. But as you enter college, something begins to shift. There's more freedom, fewer rules, and a lot more decisions to make on your own.

Welcome to **young adulthood**—where your choices start shaping your future.

This is the phase where:

- **You stop blaming and start taking responsibility.**
- **You stop waiting for motivation and start building discipline.**
- **You stop following the crowd and start figuring out who you really are.**

The biggest change?
Life no longer happens to you. You start happening to life.

In teenage years, your focus was survival—getting through classes, dealing with pressure, passing exams, and managing emotions. But in your college years, the focus should shift to **building**—your skills, your identity, your network, and your career path.

This transition won't be easy.
You'll feel lost sometimes. You'll make mistakes. You'll outgrow some friends. You'll change directions.
That's okay. That's growth.

The important thing is to **start thinking like an adult**—not just in terms of responsibilities, but in terms of mindset.

Ask yourself:

- What am I really good at?
- What do I enjoy doing even without being told?
- What kind of life do I want 5 or 10 years from now?
- What habits will take me there?

Teenagers chase trends. Young adults build trajectories.
Teenagers seek approval. Young adults seek alignment.
Teenagers want to win today. Young adults plan for tomorrow.

The world starts taking you seriously when **you** start taking your life seriously.
That shift—**from drifting to designing your future**—is the change this book is here to support.

You're not just growing older.
You're growing **wiser, stronger, and more capable**—if you choose to.

Let's grow forward.

About The Author

Dr. Ashish Gupta is a life & career coach, educator, and author who has spent over 14 years working at the intersection of higher education, student development, and personal growth. As the Director of Admissions & Outreach at RV University and the founder of multiple student-focused initiatives, he has guided thousands of young minds toward clarity, confidence, and career success.

With a deep passion for unlocking human potential, Ashish

combines practical wisdom with compassionate mentorship to help students not just choose the right path but thrive on it. His previous book, Letters to Teenagers, was a heartfelt guide for high schoolers navigating life and identity. Letters to College Students is the natural sequel—speaking directly to young adults stepping into one of the most important phases of their lives.

Whether speaking on stage, mentoring one-on-one, or writing words that feel like a conversation, Ashish's core message remains the same:
You are capable of building a life you're proud of—and it starts now.

Part 1: Foundation for Success

CHAPTER I

Own Your College Years

Dear Friend,

Let's start with a simple truth:
College can either be a turning point or a time-pass. The choice is yours.

These 3–4 years are more than just classes, grades, and assignments. They are a rare window of time in your life when:

- You have **freedom** without full responsibility
- You have **energy** without exhaustion
- You have **access** to people, resources, and opportunities without real-world barriers

In short, college is a gift. But only if you choose to **own it.**

What does it mean to "own" your college years?

It means you stop seeing college as just a place to earn a degree and start seeing it as your **launchpad**—for your career, for your personal growth, and for discovering who you are meant to become.

Let me tell you what most students do:
They enter college, go with the flow, follow the crowd, study before exams, do the bare minimum, and

suddenly—four years are gone. Then comes the regret: "I wish I had done more."

Don't let that be you.

Owning your college years means:

- **Taking Initiative:** Start things. Join clubs. Lead events. Don't just participate—contribute.
- **Exploring Interests:** Try internships. Take up side projects. Learn beyond your syllabus.
- **Building Skills:** Communication, collaboration, critical thinking, creativity—these are more important than marks.
- **Managing Time:** Learn how to balance fun and focus. Party if you want—but don't party away your potential.
- **Surrounding Yourself with Doers:** Who you spend time with will define your direction.
- **Asking for Help:** Seek mentors. Talk to faculty. Reach out to alumni. Most people are willing to help—if you ask.

And most importantly, **take ownership of your learning and your life.**
You don't need to have it all figured out. But you need to start figuring yourself out.

You have time, energy, freedom, and access right now.
Use them well. Or lose them.

One day, you'll look back at these years. Let that look be filled with pride, not regret.

Own your college years. Don't outsource them to luck or laziness.

This is your time.
Make it count.

With belief in your potential,
Ashish

CHAPTER II

Clarity is Power – Know What You Want

Dear Friend,

Let me ask you something:
If I gave you a train ticket right now—but didn't tell you where it was headed—would you get on it?
Probably not.

Yet, that's exactly how many people live their lives.
They study without knowing why. They work without knowing where it's leading. They live on autopilot, hoping life will somehow figure itself out.

Here's the hard truth:
You cannot reach a destination you've never defined.

In college, it's easy to get distracted by what everyone else is doing—placements, exams, competitions, parties, internships. You keep running... but where are you running to?

That's why this letter is about one word that will transform your journey: **Clarity.**

Why Clarity Matters

Clarity gives you:

- **Direction** – so you don't waste time or energy chasing what doesn't matter.
- **Confidence** – because you know what you're working towards.
- **Discipline** – because your daily actions are aligned with your bigger goals.

A student with average marks but clear goals will always outperform a topper who's confused.

But What If You Don't Know Yet?

That's okay.
Clarity is not something you wait for. It's something you create.

Start by asking yourself:

- What excites me?
- What am I naturally good at?
- What problems in the world do I want to solve?
- What kind of lifestyle do I want 5 or 10 years from now?
- Who are the people I admire—and why?

Write down your answers. Reflect. Talk to mentors. Explore.
And as you move forward, your vision will become clearer.

Clarity Is a Process

You don't need all the answers today.

But you must start asking the right questions.

Even a rough map is better than no map.
Your clarity will evolve—but it starts with **intentional thinking.**

Don't live someone else's dream. Don't follow the herd.
Design your path. Define your dream. Discover your purpose.

Remember:
Clarity is not a luxury. It's a necessity.
It's the difference between wandering and winning.

The earlier you gain it, the farther you'll go.

Wishing you a journey full of purpose and power,
Ashish

CHAPTER III

The Myth of the Perfect Career

Dear Friend,

Let me guess. You've probably been asked this question a hundred times already:
"So, what do you want to become?"

And every time, you feel a strange pressure—like you must have the perfect answer.
A career path that sounds impressive. A plan that feels certain. A dream that's crystal clear.

But let me tell you something I wish someone had told me earlier:
There is no such thing as a perfect career.

That's a myth.

The Reality No One Talks About

Most people don't figure it out in one go.
They try. They stumble. They change their minds. They evolve.
That's not failure—that's how real careers are built.

The world is changing too fast for "perfect."
New roles are being born every year. Entire industries are being redefined.
The job you may love in 5 years might not even exist today.

9

So don't waste your college years waiting to discover the perfect career.

Instead, **focus on becoming the kind of person who can thrive in any career.**

What to Focus On Instead

- **Learn broadly** – Explore different fields, even outside your course.
- **Build skills** – Communication, problem-solving, adaptability - these work everywhere.
- **Know your values** – What kind of work energizes you? What kind of problems do you love solving?
- **Follow your curiosity** – It will lead you to surprising places.

The truth is, your first job won't be your last. Your first passion may not be your final purpose.

And that's okay.

Your Career is a Journey, Not a Jackpot

You're not picking a career like picking a lucky lottery number.

You're building it, one step at a time—with action, reflection, and course correction.

Let go of the pressure to find "the one."

Instead, build a foundation strong enough to create many possibilities.

The most successful people I know didn't find a perfect path.
They created their path through learning, trying, failing, and growing.

You can too.

So relax. Breathe. Keep moving forward.

You don't need the perfect career plan.
You just need the courage to take the next right step.

Rooting for you,
Ashish

CHAPTER IV

Build Skills, Not Just Degrees

Dear Friend,

Let's get one thing straight:

A degree might get you an interview.
But your skills will get you the job—and help you grow.

It's easy to think that once you have a degree in hand, success will follow. But the real world doesn't work that way anymore. Companies don't hire your degree—they hire what you can do with it.

And here's the secret:
Everyone has a degree. Very few have real skills.

What Are "Skills" Anyway?

Skills are the tools in your professional toolbox. They're the things you can actually do.

Some are **technical**—like coding, design, data analysis, video editing, digital marketing, finance modeling.
Some are **soft skills**—like communication, leadership, time management, negotiation, critical thinking, creativity.

Most students focus on **scoring marks.**
Winners focus on **learning skills.**

Why Skills Matter More Than Ever

In today's world:

- Skills are the new currency.
- Skill-based hiring is replacing degree-based hiring.
- Freelancers, creators, and entrepreneurs are thriving—not because of what they studied, but because of what they can offer.

You don't need permission to build skills. You just need intention.

YouTube, LinkedIn Learning, Coursera, free blogs, side projects, internships—there are endless ways to upskill.

Start Small, Start Now

Want to stand out in college? Do this:

- Join that club and learn how to manage a team.
- Intern even if it's unpaid—learn on the job.
- Start a small blog, podcast, or YouTube channel.
- Build a simple app or website.
- Practice public speaking.
- Volunteer for an NGO and lead something.

It doesn't have to be perfect. It just has to be real.

Degree + Skills = Magic

Your degree gives you credibility.
Your skills give you capability.

Put them together, and you become unstoppable.

So don't wait for placement season to start learning.
Start now. Because when you walk into that interview room
(or startup pitch), they won't just ask what you studied.
They'll ask: **What can you do?**

And I want you to have a powerful answer.

Keep learning, keep building,
Ashish

CHAPTER V

Time is Your Greatest Asset

Dear Friend,

If I gave you ₹1 lakh right now, you'd probably be thrilled. But what if I told you that every day, life gives you something far more valuable?

Time.

You get 24 hours a day—just like the most successful people in the world.
What separates them from the rest isn't luck or genius—it's how they **use their time.**

Here's a truth that will hit you hard one day:
Time wasted in college is time borrowed from your future.

Why Time Matters More Than You Think

College feels long. But it's not.

Before you know it, final year will arrive, and the clock will feel like it's in fast forward mode.
So many students say, "I'll start later." But later never comes. And by the time they're ready to take life seriously, they've already lost years of momentum.

The most successful students I've met didn't work 24/7.

They just **respected time** more than others.

They didn't say, "I'm busy."
They asked, "What am I busy doing?"

Time is Not Just for Studying

When I say time is your greatest asset, I don't mean you should study all the time.
I mean:

- Learn something new every week
- Build something—skills, projects, relationships
- Invest time in your health
- Read, reflect, reset
- Do things that add value to your future self

Every hour you spend scrolling aimlessly, binge-watching nonsense, or procrastinating... you're silently stealing from your own dreams.

Harsh? Yes. True? Also yes.

Use Time Like an Investor

Treat your time like money.
Spend some. Save some. And most importantly—**invest some.**

Invest time in:

- Learning a new skill

- Networking with the right people
- Building your portfolio or resume
- Thinking about your future
- Developing discipline and consistency

Just 1 focused hour a day can transform your life in a year. That's not an exaggeration—it's math.

You Won't Get This Time Again
You can earn back money.
You can bounce back from failure.
But you can never get back time.

Don't let college be a blur of mindless scrolling, endless distractions, and lost opportunities.

Guard your time. Prioritize wisely. Say no to what doesn't serve your future.

And remember—your future self is depending on how you spend your time today.

Make it count.

With urgency and encouragement,
Ashish

CHAPTER VI

Be Curious, Be a Learner for Life

Dear Friend,

There's a common belief that once college ends, learning ends.
But that couldn't be further from the truth.

In reality, the most successful and fulfilled people I know have one thing in common:
They never stop learning.

They're not just students of a university—**they are students of life.**

And the fuel that drives lifelong learning?
Curiosity.

Curiosity > Intelligence

You don't need to be the smartest person in the room.
You just need to be the **most curious.**

Curious people ask questions.
They explore new ideas.
They observe the world.
They challenge their own thinking.

And as a result, they grow—faster, deeper, and in ways others don't.

College is Just the Beginning

What you learn in classrooms is important. But what will set you apart in life is what you learn outside them.

- Read books that challenge your thinking
- Watch documentaries, listen to podcasts, explore different domains
- Ask people about their journeys, their lessons, their mistakes
- Attend seminars, workshops, webinars—even if no one else does
- Say yes to learning something just because it excites you

You don't need a reason to learn something.
Curiosity is reason enough.

Lifelong Learners Win in the Long Run

The world is changing every year—new industries, new tools, new skills.
If you stop learning, you stop growing.
And if you stop growing, you slowly become irrelevant.

It's not degrees that future-proof your career.
It's your ability to keep learning.

Be the person who's always learning something new.
Be the person who's not afraid to say, "I don't know, but I'd love to find out."

Let Curiosity Lead You

Curiosity will:

- Open unexpected doors
- Lead to new passions
- Help you connect the dots across disciplines
- Make you more interesting, more skilled, and more alive

And most importantly—curiosity will make you humble. Because the more you learn, the more you realize how much you don't know.

So, stay curious.
Read widely. Listen deeply. Learn constantly.

Because in a world that's always evolving, the best learners are the ones who lead.

Keep learning,
Ashish

Part 2: Mastering the Inner Game

CHAPTER VII

Confidence Comes from Competence

Dear Friend,

We often admire confident people.
They speak boldly, walk with purpose, and seem to know exactly what they're doing.

And you might wonder—**"How can I be that confident?"**

Here's the secret most people won't tell you:
True confidence doesn't come from pretending. It comes from preparation.
It doesn't come from motivational quotes. It comes from **competence.**

What is Competence?

Competence is your ability to do something well.
It's the result of practice, knowledge, effort, and experience.

Whether it's public speaking, solving problems, coding, designing, writing, or leading a team—when you know what you're doing, you naturally feel more confident.

Because you've done the work. You've put in the reps. You've earned it.

Stop Chasing Fake Confidence

We live in a world where people are told to "just be confident" without actually becoming capable.
That's like trying to win a cricket match with just pep talk and no practice.

Confidence without competence is arrogance.
But confidence with competence? That's unstoppable.

Build Skills, Build Confidence

Want to speak with confidence in front of a crowd? Practice every week.
Want to feel confident in interviews? Learn the skill, research the company, rehearse your answers.
Want to feel confident while leading? Volunteer for leadership roles, however small.

Every hour you invest in learning, every time you push through fear and try—that's how confidence is built.

And here's the best part:
The more competent you become in one area, the more confident you feel in other areas too.

Because you begin to trust yourself.

Earn Your Confidence

Don't fake it till you make it.
Train till you trust yourself.

And the best time to start building competence is now—in

college, where you have space to try, fail, learn, and grow.

So stop waiting to "feel ready." Start getting good.
Because every skill you master becomes a new pillar of your confidence.

You don't need to shout to be confident. You just need to show up with skill.

Keep sharpening. Keep growing. Your confidence will follow.

Believing in your potential,
Ashish

CHAPTER VIII

Beat Procrastination, Win the Day

Dear Friend,

Let's be honest—**you know what needs to be done.**
But somehow... you just can't get started.

You delay it. You scroll. You tell yourself you'll do it "later."
And before you know it, the day is gone.

That, my friend, is the silent killer of college success:
procrastination.

It doesn't come with noise or alarms.
It comes with comfort. And excuses. And lies like "I work better under pressure."

The Real Cost of Procrastination

Procrastination doesn't just waste your time.
It drains your energy.
It adds anxiety to your mind.
And it quietly robs you of your **potential.**

One unfinished task leads to a guilty mind. A guilty mind leads to low motivation.
And then you're stuck in a cycle—of doing nothing, but feeling tired all the time.

You're not lazy. You're just caught in a loop.

It's time to break it.

Why We Procrastinate

We usually procrastinate when:

- The task feels too big
- We're afraid we won't do it perfectly
- We don't feel motivated
- We think we have "plenty of time"

But here's the truth:
You don't need motivation. You need momentum.

Small Wins Create Big Progress

Start small. Start messy. Start afraid.
But start.

Here's what works:

- Break big tasks into micro-tasks
- Use the 5-minute rule: "I'll just do this for 5 minutes"
- Remove distractions (yes, put the phone away)
- Set timers and reward yourself
- Finish one important task before checking social media

Every time you win over procrastination, even in small ways, you build **discipline.**
And discipline beats motivation. Every. Single. Time.

Imagine the Compound Effect

If you beat procrastination for just one hour a day...
That's 365 hours a year. That's more than 15 full days of
focused work.

What could you build in that time?
A new skill? A business idea? A stronger you?

Procrastination delays your dreams.
Discipline delivers them.

So the next time you feel the urge to postpone, pause and
ask yourself:
*"Will this action move me closer to my future—or keep me
stuck?"*

You don't have to be perfect.
You just have to win the day. One task at a time.

Let's go. The clock is ticking.

With urgency and belief,
Ashish

CHAPTER IX

Your Mindset Shapes Your Future

Dear Friend,

Here's something I've learned after years of working with students, professionals, and entrepreneurs:

It's not talent. Not intelligence. Not even opportunity.
The real game-changer is your **mindset.**

Your mindset is the lens through which you see the world. And the lens you choose determines what you believe, how you act, and ultimately—**who you become.**

Two Kinds of Mindsets

Psychologist Carol Dweck describes two mindsets that shape everything:

1. **Fixed Mindset** – Believes "I am who I am. I can't change much."
This mindset fears failure, avoids challenges, and gives up easily.

2. **Growth Mindset** – Believes "I can learn, improve, and grow."
This mindset embraces challenges, learns from failure, and keeps evolving.

Now ask yourself:

Which one are you living with?

Your Beliefs Become Your Reality

If you believe you're "not good at math," you won't even try.
If you believe you "can't speak confidently," you'll avoid every opportunity to practice.
But the truth is: **You are not your current ability—you are your potential.**

And your potential is expandable.
But only if you believe it is.

How to Develop a Growth Mindset

- Replace "I can't do this" with "I can't do this yet."
- See failures as feedback, not defeat
- Stop comparing—start competing with your past self
- Surround yourself with growth-minded people
- Celebrate effort, not just outcomes

Every time you choose growth over comfort, your mindset strengthens.

Your Mindset, Your Future

College is not just about learning subjects.
It's about learning how to **think.**

And if you train your mind to:

- Look for solutions, not excuses
- Stay calm during chaos
- Focus on progress, not perfection
- Believe in effort, not luck

You'll be ready for anything life throws at you.

Because here's the ultimate truth:
Your mindset is the foundation on which your future is built.

Upgrade it. Every day.

Rooting for your growth,
Ashish

CHAPTER X

Resilience – The Hidden Superpower

Dear Friend,

Life won't always go as planned.
You'll face rejection.
You'll lose people.
You'll fail—sometimes publicly, sometimes silently.
And in those moments, you'll ask:
"Why me?"

Here's the truth I want you to hold onto:
It's not what happens to you that defines you—it's how you respond.

And that response?
It's called resilience.

What is Resilience?

Resilience is not about being tough all the time.
It's not about pretending everything is fine.
Resilience is the quiet strength to bend without breaking.
To fall, and rise. To feel pain, but not quit.

It's your **hidden superpower**—the one you discover only when life tests you.

College Will Test You

There will be moments when:

- You study hard but still fall short
- You don't get that internship, role, or recognition
- You feel stuck, lost, or behind everyone else
- Things go wrong despite your best efforts

It's normal. It's part of growing up.

But here's what most students don't realize—
These struggles are not obstacles. They are training.

They're building your emotional muscles.
They're teaching you how to stay calm in chaos.
They're shaping you into someone who can handle the real world with strength and grace.

How to Build Resilience

- **Feel, but don't freeze.** It's okay to feel disappointed—but don't let it paralyze you.
- **Reflect, don't overthink.** Ask: What did I learn? How can I grow from this?
- **Lean on your circle.** Talk to someone. Don't suffer in silence.
- **Bounce back with action.** Even a small step forward is a victory.
- **Remember your "why."** Purpose fuels perseverance.

Resilience is like a muscle—it grows only when tested.
Every setback, every low moment, every "I can't do this"

day—it's all part of the process.

And one day, you'll look back and realize:
It wasn't the easy days that made you strong. It was the hard ones.

You don't have to be fearless. You just have to be unbreakable.

Stay strong, bounce back, and keep moving forward.

With deep belief in your strength,
Ashish

CHAPTER XI

Don't Compare, Create Your Own Path

Dear Friend,

It starts silently.
You scroll through Instagram and see a classmate getting an internship at a top company.
Someone else is launching a startup. Another just posted their GRE score.
And suddenly, without meaning to, you begin to feel like **you're behind.**

Let me tell you something important:
Comparison is the fastest way to kill your joy—and your journey.

The Trap of Comparison

We've all been there.
Looking at someone else's highlight reel and comparing it to our behind-the-scenes.
But here's the thing:

- Everyone is walking a different path
- Everyone has their own pace, their own pain, their own process
- And most people are only sharing their best moments—not their breakdowns

You're not behind.
You're just on **your own path.**

Create, Don't Compare

You weren't born to be a copy of someone else.
You were born to **create your own version of success**—on your own terms.

What excites you?
What kind of life do you want?
What strengths do you have that others don't?

Instead of comparing your Chapter 3 to someone else's Chapter 20, focus on **writing your own story well.**

Comparison creates pressure.
Creation brings purpose.

Shift Your Focus

From envy to **empathy** – Admire people, but understand they have struggles too

From fear to **focus** – You don't need to be everywhere. Just be present where you are

From chasing applause to **chasing alignment** – Do what feels right, not what looks good online

Your path may be slower. It may be quieter. It may not look "glamorous" right now.

But if it's authentic, if it's yours—it's powerful.

Stay Rooted in Your Journey

There's only one person you need to compete with:
The person you were yesterday.

If you're growing, evolving, and staying true to yourself—you're doing just fine.

So breathe. Log off if you need to. Focus on building, not comparing.

The world doesn't need another copy.
It needs the original story only you can write.

Walk your path—with confidence.

Always cheering for you,
Ashish

Part 3: Building Career Capital

CHAPTER XII

Communication Will Make or Break You

Dear Friend,

You may be brilliant.
You may have the best ideas.
You may even have top grades, certifications, and skills.

But if you can't **communicate** them well—clearly, confidently, and convincingly—
the world will never know your true potential.

Let's face it:
In the real world, it's not just about what you know.
It's about how well you can **express** what you know.

Communication is a Career Superpower

- Great communicators:
- Get hired faster
- Lead better
- Build stronger relationships
- Handle conflicts maturely
- And stand out in every room they walk into

Whether it's writing an email, cracking an interview, leading a team, presenting an idea, networking at an event, or even just expressing your thoughts—**communication is the bridge between you and success.**

But Here's the Good News

You're not born with it—you **build** it.
And college is the best time to do that.

Start small:

- Speak up in class
- Join a debate or theater club
- Start a YouTube channel or podcast
- Write LinkedIn posts or blogs
- Practice interviews with friends
- Read aloud, record yourself, watch talks by great speakers

Like any skill, the more you practice, the more confident you become.

Don't Just Learn English. Learn to Express

It's not about speaking in "perfect English." It's about:

- Being clear, not complicated
- Being real, not robotic
- Being structured, not scattered
- Being confident, not cocky

Communication is not about fancy words. It's about

authentic connection.

In the End, People Remember…

Not just your knowledge, but your **voice.**
Not just your resume, but your **presence.**
Not just your degree, but your **ability to connect and convey.**

So take it seriously. Work on it daily.

Because in a crowded world, your communication is your differentiation.

Speak with clarity. Write with confidence. Communicate with purpose.

It will take you places your qualifications alone never could.

To your voice being heard,
Ashish

CHAPTER XIII

Build a Personal Brand Early

Dear Friend,

You may think **"personal branding"** is something for influencers, entrepreneurs, or CEOs.
But here's the truth:
You already have a personal brand—whether you've built it intentionally or not.

Your personal brand is nothing but the way people **perceive you,** talk about you, and remember you when you're not in the room.

And in today's hyper-connected world, where opportunities often come through people and platforms—not just degrees—your personal brand can open doors before your resume even arrives.

Why Start in College?

Because this is the perfect time to:

- Explore your interests
- Showcase your work
- Build your voice
- And stand out in a crowd full of sameness

College is not just a place to prepare for the job market—it's a place to **position yourself** in it.

What Is Your Brand Saying?

Ask yourself:

- What am I known for in my circle?
- What do people come to me for help with?
- What does my online presence say about me?
- Do I have a digital footprint that reflects my interests and abilities?

If you're not defining your brand, others are doing it for you—based on limited information or outdated impressions.

How to Build Your Personal Brand (Practically)

1. **Identify Your Strength Zone**
   What do you want to be known for—design, finance, writing, leadership, tech, storytelling?
2. **Create Valuable Content**
   Share what you're learning. Start a blog, LinkedIn profile, YouTube channel, or even a newsletter.
   Don't overthink—just start sharing your journey.
3. **Show, Don't Just Tell**
   Instead of saying "I'm passionate about marketing," show a campaign you worked on.
   Instead of saying, "I'm a great communicator," share a video of you speaking.
4. **Be Consistent**
   Your brand isn't built in a week. Show up regularly,

refine your voice, and keep improving.

5. **Stay Authentic**
   Your brand isn't a performance. It's your reputation. Build it on truth, not trends.

Remember: Visibility Creates Opportunity

When people know who you are and what you stand for, they remember you.
And when the right opportunity comes up—you're already top of mind.

Your degree might help you get noticed.
But your personal brand will make you unforgettable.

So don't wait to graduate to build it.
Start today. Grow with it. And let it speak for you—loudly and proudly.

You are your brand. Make it worth following.

With purpose and power,
Ashish

CHAPTER XIV

Internships Are More Important Than You Think

Dear Friend,

Let's talk about something that most students underestimate—and later regret not taking seriously:

Internships.

To many, internships are just something to "add to the resume."
But in reality, they are so much more.

An internship can give you what your classroom often can't:
Exposure. Experience. Exploration.

Why Internships Matter So Much

Because they help you:

- Understand how the real world works
- Apply what you've learned in class to real problems
- Build your professional network early
- Discover what you do and don't enjoy doing
- Gain the confidence to speak in interviews—not with theory, but with experience

Here's the deal:
Employers today don't just want degrees—they want proof of performance.
Internships are that proof.

Think Beyond the Stipend

Yes, paid internships are great. But don't say no to a good opportunity just because it doesn't pay.
Sometimes the **right learning, mentorship, or exposure is** far more valuable than a few thousand rupees.

Treat every internship like an investment in your future.

How to Make the Most of Your Internship

- Show up with energy, even if it's remote or part-time
- Ask questions, take initiative, be the one who's remembered
- Network with your colleagues—every connection counts
- Reflect on what you're learning and where you're growing
- Add your work to a portfolio—not just your resume

Remember: An average student with 2–3 solid internships will often beat a topper with none.

Start Early, Explore Widely

First-year? Start exploring roles.

Second-year? Get hands-on experience.
Third-year? Get serious about industry fit.
Final-year? Intern with the intention to convert it into a job offer.

The earlier you start, the clearer your future becomes.

So don't wait for "the right time."
Start interning. Start learning. Start building your edge.

Because in the real world, **experience isn't optional—it's essential.**

Intern smart. Intern often. And let your career begin before you graduate.

Wishing you a career full of meaningful work,
Ashish

CHAPTER XV

Learn to Network Without Feeling Fake

Dear Friend,

Let's admit it—
The word **"networking"** often feels awkward, uncomfortable, or even fake.

It brings to mind forced conversations, awkward LinkedIn messages, or people pretending to be interested just to get ahead.

But here's the truth:
Networking isn't about using people. It's about connecting with people.
Real people. With real experiences. And real value to share.

Why Networking Matters—Especially in College

Your degree gives you knowledge.
Your skills give you confidence.
But your **network?** That's what often gives you **opportunities.**

From internships to job referrals, collaborations to mentorship—many of the best career breaks come not from job portals, but from people.

But I Don't Want to Be "Fake"

Good. You shouldn't be.
Because **authentic networking is not about impressing—it's about connecting.**

Here's how you can do that:

1. Be Curious, Not Clever
Ask people about their journey. Learn from their experience. People love to share if you genuinely care.

2. Give Before You Ask
Share a resource, promote their work, offer to help.
Even a simple "I really enjoyed your article/talk/post" can be a great way to start.

3. Use Platforms Smartly
LinkedIn, college events, workshops, webinars—these are goldmines of connection. Don't just scroll. Engage. Comment. DM thoughtfully.

4. Follow Up, Don't Fade Out
A connection is like a plant—it needs nurturing. Follow up after meetings. Keep the relationship warm, not transactional.

5. Your Seniors Are Your Hidden Network
Reach out to alumni. Ask about their college-to-career journey. Most of them are happy to help if you're respectful and curious.

Networking Is a Skill, Not a Trick

You don't need to be an extrovert. You just need to be **intentional and respectful.**

Speak with purpose. Listen with attention. Follow up with gratitude.

Over time, your network becomes your **circle of growth**—people who guide you, challenge you, support you, and open doors you didn't even know existed.

Remember This:

**Opportunities often flow through relationships.
And relationships begin with a simple hello.**

So start today. Reach out. Stay genuine. Be kind.
And build your network before you need it.

The connections you build now might change your life later.

Cheering for your growth,
Ashish

CHAPTER XVI

College Projects Can Launch Careers

Dear Friend,

When most students hear the word "college project," they think of:

- Copy-pasting from the internet
- Submitting something just to get marks
- Doing it at the last minute with minimum effort

But let me tell you something that can shift your perspective completely:

Your college project can be the start of your career.
Yes—**if done right**, it can be more than just an assignment. It can become your **portfolio**, your **startup idea**, your **internship pitch**, or even your **first job offer.**

The Problem? Most Students Waste the Opportunity

They see projects as a task. Not as a chance.
They do what's required. Not what's possible.

But every project—whether it's a research paper, business plan, tech build, case study, or creative piece—is your sandbox to explore, experiment, and express your talent.

Here's How to Turn Projects Into Career Capital

1. Pick Topics That Genuinely Interest You
Don't just choose what's easy. Choose what excites you, challenges you, or aligns with your future goals.

2. Go Beyond What's Expected
Add original research. Build a prototype. Record a presentation. Interview people. Show effort.

3. Document & Showcase It
Turn your project into a SlideShare, LinkedIn post, blog, YouTube video, or portfolio entry. Let the world see what you can do.

4. Use It to Start Conversations
Your project can be a great icebreaker when networking or interviewing. It shows initiative, passion, and practical thinking.

5. Collaborate With Serious Teammates
Good projects are built by people who care. Choose your team wisely—or be the leader who makes everyone care.

Real Careers Have Been Launched From Classrooms

- Students have started startups from final-year projects.
- Others landed jobs because they showcased a brilliant marketing or coding assignment.
- Some discovered their passion just by going deep into a subject they picked for a small class project.

The point is—your college work doesn't have to end in a

file.
It can be the beginning of something real.

Marks Fade. Mastery Stays.

Anyone can complete an assignment.
But few own their project, go the extra mile, and turn it into
a **statement of skill.**

Be that person.

Because the world doesn't just want degrees—it wants
doers.
And your college project is a great place to start **doing.**

Build with intention,
Ashish

CHAPTER XVII

Digital Presence Matters – Use It Wisely

Dear Friend,

Let me ask you a simple question:

If someone Googled your name today, what would they find?

In a world where almost everything is digital, your online presence isn't optional—it's your first impression.

Before recruiters meet you, before collaborators reach out, even before someone responds to your internship email—they often do one thing:
They check you out online.

And in that moment, your digital presence either speaks **for you**... or works **against you.**

You Are Already Online. The Only Question Is—What's the Story?

Your Instagram, your Twitter, your LinkedIn, your YouTube channel, your blog, your comments—
They all tell the world who you are and what you care about.

So here's the rule:
Be intentional. Be professional. Be real.

Build a Digital Presence That Works for You

1. Clean Up What Doesn't Reflect You Well
You don't have to delete everything—but do ask:
"Does this post/comment align with who I want to be known as?"

2. Create a Solid LinkedIn Profile
A professional display picture. Clear summary. Your projects, skills, and aspirations.
Start building your digital resume.

3. Showcase Your Work

- If you write, publish articles
- If you design, share your portfolio
- If you speak, upload a video
- If you learn, reflect through posts

4. Engage With Intention
Comment meaningfully. Follow thought leaders. Join online communities related to your field.

5. Google Yourself Regularly
It may sound silly, but it shows you what others see—and helps you stay in control of your online image.

Use Social Media to Build, Not Just Scroll

Social media can be a powerful tool—**if you use it mindfully.**

- Learn from it
- Connect through it
- Share your journey on it
- Use it to grow—not just to be seen

Let people see you as a learner, a thinker, a doer—not just a consumer of trends.

You Are Your Digital Footprint

You can either let your digital presence happen by accident...
Or you can **design it with intention.**

Start now.
Because one day, your online presence might be the reason you get your dream opportunity—or miss it.

The internet remembers.
Make sure it remembers you for the right reasons.

Use it wisely,
Ashish

CHAPTER XVIII

Start Something – Anything!

Dear Friend,

If there's one habit that separates the doers from the dreamers in college, it's this:

They start.

While most students wait—
For the right time,
For more confidence,
For someone to tell them it's okay...

The ones who grow fastest are the ones who **start something—anything.**

A blog.
A YouTube channel.
A podcast.
A coding project.
A campus club.
A newsletter.
A community initiative.
A social media page.
A mini startup.
A research paper.
Even a side hustle that fails.

Because here's the truth:

You don't need permission to begin. You just need the courage to start.

Why Starting Early Matters

- When you start something of your own:
- You learn more than any textbook could teach
- You discover your real strengths
- You build leadership, problem-solving, creativity
- You learn how to deal with feedback, failure, and growth
- You stand out from 99% of students who just attend classes

Even if it doesn't go viral, or make money, or last forever—**it makes you better.**

"But I Don't Know What to Start..."

Perfect. That's the best place to begin.

Start small. Start messy. Start curious.
The goal is not to get it right—it's to get it going.

- Still unsure? Try this:
- What frustrates you? Solve it.
- What excites you? Share it.
- What do you wish existed? Build it.
- What are you learning? Document it.

You don't need a team, funds, or a 50-slide pitch deck.
You just need action.

Done is Better Than Perfect

Don't overthink. Don't wait till you feel "ready."
No one's ready the first time.

But those who start become ready while doing.

Some of the world's best creators, founders, and professionals started in college—with ideas that looked silly to others but made sense to them.

They didn't wait. They **acted.** And you can too.

Build Your Story Before the World Asks For It

In your future interviews, pitches, or networking moments, imagine being able to say:
"Yes, I started something in college—and here's what I learned from it."

That sentence alone can set you apart.

So go ahead. Start something.

Not because you have to...
But because you **can**—and you'll grow from it.

Your journey begins with one step.
Take it.

Starting with belief in you, **Ashish**

Part 4: Choices, Challenges & Character

CHAPTER XIX

How to Make the Right Career Decisions

Dear Friend,

At some point during college—maybe it's today, maybe it's tomorrow—you'll find yourself asking:

"What should I do with my life?"
"Which career is right for me?"
"What if I make the wrong choice?"

Let me start by saying this:
You're not alone.
Everyone—even the most successful people—have faced this confusion.

Because career decisions aren't just about a job.
They're about **who you are, what matters to you, and where you want your life to go.**

There's No One "Right" Career

Let's bust the myth right away:
There is no perfect career waiting out there for you to magically discover.
There are only **good choices, made intentionally, followed by consistent action.**

You don't need all the answers now.
But you do need a process to make better decisions.

Here it is.

1. Know Yourself First

Before asking what career, ask:

- What excites me?
- What kind of problems do I love solving?
- Do I prefer structure or creativity?
- Do I enjoy working with people or ideas?
- What skills come naturally to me?

Clarity begins with self-awareness.

2. Explore, Don't Just Assume

Don't choose careers based on what others are doing, what looks glamorous, or what your relatives say.

Intern. Volunteer. Talk to people in the field. Watch interviews. Try projects.

Treat career exploration like dating—you don't commit without understanding.

3. Align Career With Values

Ask:

- What kind of lifestyle do I want?
- How important is money, freedom, impact, status, or stability to me?
- Am I okay with a high-pressure job or do I prefer a balanced life?

A career aligned with your values will bring satisfaction, not just success.

4. Skills Over Titles

Focus on **what you'll learn**, not just what you'll be called.

A role that challenges you and helps you grow is often more valuable than one that just "sounds good."

5. No Decision is Permanent

Here's the truth:
You can change your mind.
You can pivot. You can evolve.

The first job, course, or career path you choose isn't a life sentence—it's a starting point.

Every step teaches you something. Nothing is wasted.

6. Talk to the Right People

Find mentors. Speak to seniors. Connect with professionals. Ask real questions:

- What's your day like?

- What do you love and hate about your job?
- If you were starting now, what would you do differently?

Wisdom from experience can save you years of confusion.

7. Decide With Courage, Not Fear

Don't choose safety over growth.
Don't say yes to something just because you're scared to say no.

The right decision may feel uncomfortable now but will empower you in the long run.

In the End, Ask Yourself This:

Will this path help me grow into the person I want to become?

If the answer is yes—even with some fear and uncertainty—you're on the right track.

You don't need the perfect plan.
You just need to take the next best step with intention.

And remember:
The most successful careers aren't chosen once—they're built continuously.

So, start building yours.

With clarity and confidence, **Ashish**

CHAPTER XX

Handling Rejections and Failures

Dear Friend,

Let's talk about something no one likes to experience—
but **everyone** goes through:
Rejection and failure.

You didn't get selected for the internship.
Your name wasn't on the placement list.
Your idea got rejected.
Your marks weren't good enough.
You tried... and still, things didn't go your way.

It hurts. I get it.
But I want you to hear this loud and clear:

Failure is not the opposite of success.
It's part of the process that leads to success.

Everyone Fails. You're Not Alone.

Behind every successful person, there's a trail of:

- Emails that were ignored
- Interviews that didn't go well
- Ideas that flopped
- Days when they felt like giving up

What separates them isn't luck or talent.
It's **how they responded to failure.**

Here's What Rejection Really Means

- It's redirection—not the end
- It's feedback—not a final judgment
- It's a moment—not your identity

You didn't fail. **You learned what doesn't work.**
And that's powerful.

How to Handle Failure Like a Pro

1. **Feel it, but don't stay stuck in it**
   It's okay to feel disappointed. Allow yourself to process it. Then get back up.
2. **Ask: What did I learn?**
   Every failure has a lesson—about your preparation, mindset, or strategy.
3. **Separate outcome from effort**
   Just because something didn't work out doesn't mean you are a failure. You are evolving.
4. **Try again—with better insight**
   Make adjustments. Seek feedback. Apply again. Improve.
5. **Talk to someone**
   Don't bottle it up. A conversation with a mentor, friend, or parent can offer new perspective.

Rejection Builds Character

Here's the truth:
The more rejections you face and overcome, the more **resilient, focused, and humble** you become.

Failure tests your patience.
Rejection sharpens your hunger.
Both make your success more meaningful.

You Only Truly Fail When You Stop Trying

So the next time you get a "no," remind yourself:
This isn't the end. It's a stepping stone.
And sometimes, a rejection is life's way of saying: "Something better is coming."

Your job is to stay in the game. Keep learning. Keep showing up.

Because those who succeed are not those who never fall—
They are the ones who **always rise back up.**

Fail forward. And keep going.

With strength and solidarity,
Ashish

CHAPTER XXI

Ethics Matter – Even in College

Dear Friend,

Let's talk about something that rarely makes it to college discussions but quietly shapes the kind of person—and professional—you become:

Ethics.

In simple words, ethics is about doing the **right thing,** even when no one is watching.
It's about living with **integrity, honesty, and responsibility**—in your thoughts, choices, and actions.

You might think, *"Come on, I'm just a student. How much do ethics matter at this stage?"*

My answer:
They matter more than you think.

Because What You Practice in College... You Carry into Life

- If you copy in exams, you learn to cheat the system
- If you take shortcuts in projects, you develop habits of mediocrity
- If you lie on your resume, you start your career on shaky ground

- If you gossip, manipulate, or blame—you become someone people can't trust

Character isn't built when you get a job.
It's built right now—in your college years.

Ethics Are Not Just About Rules—They're About Reputation

Your professors, peers, seniors, and mentors are all watching—not to judge, but to **see how you show up.**

And here's the thing:
People may forget your grades, but they'll never forget your character.

Being ethical doesn't make you weak. It makes you trustworthy.
And trust is a rare currency in today's world.

What Ethical Behavior Looks Like in College

- Submitting work that's truly your own
- Acknowledging your mistakes without blaming others
- Giving credit to teammates fairly
- Keeping promises and deadlines
- Respecting different viewpoints—even when you disagree
- Doing the right thing—even if no one is clapping

The Long-Term View

You're not just building a career.
You're building a **reputation**, a **legacy,** and most importantly—a **conscience.**

In a world obsessed with results, choose to focus on how you get them.

Your talent may get you opportunities.
But your ethics will determine how long you keep them.

So be the kind of student who's not just skilled—but solid.
Not just successful—but sincere.
Not just known—but respected.

Because in the end, **what you do matters—but how you do it matters even more.**

With hope for the honest path,
Ashish

CHAPTER XXII

Friends, Relationships & Distractions

Dear Friend,

Let's get real.
College is not just about academics, projects, and placements.

It's also about **friendships, crushes, late-night conversations, heartbreaks, FOMO, and distractions**—plenty of them.

And while these things are a **natural part of the college experience**, they can either **shape you or shake you**—depending on how you handle them.

Your Circle Shapes Your Direction

Let's start with friends.

College friendships can become your strongest support system—or your biggest source of regret.
The people you hang out with influence your:

- Mindset
- Habits
- Energy
- Goals

- And even your self-worth

So choose wisely.

Ask yourself:

- Do my friends push me to grow or pull me into drama?
- Can we talk about ideas, goals, and real life—or just gossip?
- Are they there for me in tough times—or only for the fun?

You don't need a big group. You need a few real ones.
The right friends are not just company. They are compass.

Relationships: A Beautiful Mess?

Yes, love happens in college. And yes, it can be amazing.
But it can also become a **distraction, a source of emotional turbulence,** or even **a detour from your goals**—if not handled with maturity.

Before entering a relationship, ask:

- Are we adding value to each other's life?
- Can we grow together without losing our individuality?
- Are we both emotionally ready to handle the ups and downs?

Love should inspire you, not drain you.
And remember: the most important relationship is the one you have with yourself.

The Distraction Dilemma

Social media, binge-watching, endless scrolling, parties, peer pressure—distractions are everywhere.

And no, I'm not saying you should live like a monk.
But you must learn to **set boundaries.**

- Enjoy, but don't escape into distractions.
- Rest, but don't use "self-care" as an excuse for laziness.
- Be social, but don't forget your personal priorities.

Time is your most precious asset. Protect it.

Balance Is the Real Flex

The students who win in college are not the ones who avoid all fun.
They're the ones who **balance growth and enjoyment.**
Who know when to say yes—and when to say no.
Who hang out on weekends but show up strong on Monday.

Because while memories are important, so is momentum.

Choose your people. Guard your peace. Manage your energy.

Make sure your friendships and relationships help you grow, not slow you down.

Live with heart—but lead with wisdom.

With balance and belief,
Ashish

CHAPTER XXIII

Choose Mentors, Not Just Marks

Dear Friend,

College is designed to give you marks, grades, and degrees. But what it **doesn't promise**—and what actually makes the biggest difference—is this:

Mentorship.

A mentor is someone who sees your potential even when you don't.
Someone who gives you not just answers—but better questions.
Someone who helps you connect the dots between where you are and where you can go.

In short: **A good mentor can accelerate your growth more than any textbook.**

Why Mentors Matter More Than Ever

In a world full of noise, opinions, and pressure, a mentor becomes:

- Your mirror
- Your guide
- Your compass
- Your challenger
- Your quiet support system

They don't sugarcoat. They don't compete.
They invest in you—with time, experience, and honest feedback.

While your classmates are chasing marks, be the one who's building **wisdom.**
Because marks fade. But mentorship lasts.

How to Find a Mentor

It's not about waiting for someone to announce, "I will now mentor you."
It's about being **intentional:**

Look for someone a few years ahead of you—seniors, alumni, professors, or professionals.

- Observe who inspires you—**not just by success, but by values.**
- Reach out. Ask thoughtful questions. **Show curiosity.**
- Be consistent and respectful. **Don't just take—build a relationship.**

Good mentors don't want followers.
They want **learners**—people who act on advice and come back better.

Be Coachable

Mentorship only works when you're willing to:

- Listen deeply
- Accept feedback without ego
- Try new things
- Ask more than you answer

Don't look for someone to tell you what to do.
Look for someone who helps you think better, reflect deeper, and decide smarter.

And Someday... Be a Mentor

The best way to honor your mentor is to **become one** for someone else.
Share what you've learned. Uplift someone younger. Pass the torch forward.

Because in the end, success is not just about reaching the top.
It's about **lifting others as you climb.**

So, while others chase grades and awards, build relationships with people who shape your thinking.

Find your mentors. Learn deeply. Grow consistently.

That's how real progress begins.

With respect for the guides who shape us,
Ashish

Part 5: Your Road Ahead

CHAPTER XXIV

Job vs. Startup vs. Higher Studies – What's Right for You?

Dear Friend,

As you move toward the end of college, one big question starts knocking louder:
"What next?"

Should you take up a job?
Should you go for higher studies?
Or should you take the leap and start your own venture?

Everyone has an opinion.
Your parents, your peers, your professors—and yes, even your Instagram feed.

But here's what I want you to remember:
This isn't about what's "best." It's about what's right for you.

Let's break it down—honestly and practically.

1. The Job Route: Learn, Earn, Grow

Jobs give you structure, stability, and a chance to understand how the professional world works.

A good first job can help you:

- Build skills
- Gain industry exposure
- Understand workplace dynamics
- Save money or support your family
- Discover what kind of work excites you

When to choose a job:

- If you want financial independence quickly
- If you're unsure what to do long-term and want to explore
- If you want to build industry experience before making a bigger move

But remember—don't just take any job. Choose one that helps you grow, even if the salary isn't huge at first.

2. The Startup Route: Risk, Responsibility & Reward

Starting something of your own is exciting—but it's not for everyone.
It requires **clarity, courage, commitment—and a high tolerance for uncertainty.**

But the lessons? Invaluable.

You'll learn:

- How to think like a problem-solver
- How to manage chaos
- How to lead, build, fail, and start again

- More in 6 months than most people learn in 3 years

When to choose a startup path:

- If you have a problem you deeply care about solving
- If you're okay with failure and learning the hard way
- If you'd rather create something from scratch than follow existing paths

Startups aren't just about making money. They're about making meaning.
Start small. Stay lean. Stay hungry.

3. Higher Studies: Deepen Your Expertise

Higher education can be a great investment—if you know why you're doing it.

Pursue it:

- To gain specialization in your field
- To switch careers (MBA, MS, Law, Design, etc.)
- To access global opportunities or research roles
- To study under thought leaders and expand your worldview

But don't go for a master's degree just to buy time or escape pressure.
It's a costly decision—so take it consciously.

Prepare. Research. Talk to alumni. Know what doors it will open.

A Few Truths to Guide You

There's **no one-size-fits-all**. One person's dream path might be your worst nightmare.

You can **change paths** later. Many entrepreneurs start as employees. Many job-holders launch startups later.

Experimentation is allowed. Your twenties are for exploring—not for locking yourself in a box.

Whatever you choose, do it with **intention, not impulse.**

Ask Yourself Honestly:

- What excites me more—stability or building from scratch?
- Do I want to specialize or generalize right now?
- What are my current responsibilities—personal, financial, emotional?
- Am I making this decision out of passion—or pressure?
- Clarity comes from asking the right questions—not from copying others.

Your career is not a race. It's a journey.
You're allowed to walk, run, pause, and pivot.

What matters most is not where you start—but that you start with **self-awareness and a willingness to grow.**

Choose with courage,
Ashish

CHAPTER XXV

Start Preparing for Life After College Today

Dear Friend,

College feels like a bubble.
Your world revolves around classes, assignments, group projects, canteen hangouts, and last-minute submissions.

But one day soon, that bubble will burst.
The real world will arrive—with questions like:

"Where are you headed next?"

"What do you bring to the table?"

"Are you ready?"

The good news?
You don't have to wait for that day to prepare.
You can—and should—start today.

Why Wait Until You're Pushed?

Most students start preparing for life after college **only when college ends.**
By then, it's often too late to build the skills, clarity, network, or experience that give you a head start.

But if you begin now—**even in small ways**—you'll feel more confident, more capable, and more in control of your future.

What Preparation Looks Like (Practically)

1. Build Your Resume While You Study
Internships, volunteer work, campus roles, personal projects—all of it counts.
Don't wait for final year to start adding value to your profile.

2. Sharpen Your Skills Beyond Syllabus
Communication, problem-solving, digital tools, personal branding—these are what employers and the world are really looking for.

3. Start Your LinkedIn Journey
Build your profile. Connect with alumni. Share what you're learning. The digital world is where opportunities start.

4. Work on Your Clarity
Explore your career interests. Try different things. Talk to people in the field. Find mentors. Ask questions.

5. Create a Portfolio
Design student? Start showcasing your work. Writer? Blog it. Developer? Put your code online.
Whatever you're building—document and share it.

6. Understand How the Real World Works
Read about industries, startups, the economy, personal finance, and hiring trends.

This awareness will help you make better choices.

Mindset Shift: From Campus to Career

From "marks" → to **mastery**

From "attendance" → to **accountability**

From "group work" → to **ownership**

From "doing what's needed" → to **doing what builds you**

Start acting like a professional even before you become one. Dress a little sharper. Speak a little clearer. Plan a little better.

Not because someone's watching—but because **your future deserves the best version of you.**

What You Do Today... Reflects Tomorrow

You don't have to figure it all out right now.
But every small step today—every book read, skill learned, connection made, habit developed—**compounds into career capital.**

So while you enjoy these college years (and you should), don't forget to build your launchpad.

Because one day soon, the question won't be, *"What did you study?"*
It will be:

"What have you built?"
"What can you offer?"
"Are you ready?"

Start becoming that person—today.

Rooting for your future,
Ashish

CHAPTER XXVI

Purpose Over Paycheck – What Really Matters

Dear Friend,

Let's be honest—when you think about your future, money is a big part of the picture.
And that's okay.
We all want financial freedom, stability, and a life of comfort.

But here's a lesson many people learn a little too late in life:

A high paycheck without a sense of purpose will always leave you feeling empty.

Money is important—but it's not everything.
And chasing only the paycheck, without aligning it to your values, interests, or contribution to the world, is a shortcut to burnout, boredom, or breakdown.

So What is "Purpose"?

Purpose is the answer to the question:
"Why am I doing what I'm doing?"

It's not always about changing the world.
Sometimes, it's about doing work that:

- Energizes you
- Uses your strengths
- Serves people
- Aligns with what you believe in

It's waking up excited—not just to earn, but to create, contribute, and grow.

Paycheck Feeds You. Purpose Fuels You.

Here's what I've seen:

- People with purpose work harder without burning out
- They bounce back faster from failure
- They stay more driven, disciplined, and fulfilled
- They inspire others, build meaningful careers, and often earn well in the long run too

And most importantly—they feel at peace with themselves.

So What Should You Choose?

Here's the truth:
You don't have to choose between purpose and paycheck.
You just need to make sure that money is the byproduct of value you enjoy creating.

If a job pays well but kills your spirit, ask yourself:

- Is this sustainable?
- Can I grow in this?

- Am I just surviving, or thriving?

And if you're following your passion but feel financially stuck, ask:

- How can I upskill or reposition this into something valuable to others?
- What do people need that I can offer with purpose?

College Is the Best Time to Find Your "Why"

Explore different paths. Reflect on what matters to you. Don't rush to pick the highest-paying job. Pick the one that lets you **become who you want to be.**

It's not idealism. It's strategy.

Because the most successful people aren't just chasing checks.
They're chasing **challenges that matter** to them.
And money follows them—not the other way around.

A Final Thought:

The world doesn't just need more professionals.
It needs more people who are alive, awake, and aligned with what they do.

So yes—earn well. But don't forget to live well.

And remember, a meaningful life is built not by the size of

your salary...
But by the depth of your purpose.

Lead with purpose. Let the paycheck follow.

With heart and hope,
Ashish

CHAPTER XXVII

You Are Building a Life, Not Just a Career

Dear Friend,

In college, it's easy to get caught up in career talk.

Placements. Packages. Profiles. Promotions.

And while there's nothing wrong with being ambitious—here's a gentle reminder I hope you carry with you:

You are not just building a career.
You are building a life.

A career is a big part of your life—but it's not the only part.

Because when the laptop shuts down, the meeting ends, or the day's work is done...
It's your relationships, your health, your values, your inner peace, and your memories that matter most.

Define Success Your Way

Don't let society define what success should look like for you.
For some, it's a high-paying job in a big city.
For others, it's peaceful work in their hometown.

For some, it's entrepreneurship.
For others, it's service, teaching, creating, or exploring.

There's no one formula.
Only alignment with what feels true to you.

A Full Life Has Many Dimensions

While building your career, don't forget to also build:

- **Relationships** – Friends, family, mentors. People who make life worth living.
- **Health** – Physical, mental, emotional. Without it, no success matters.
- **Passions** – Hobbies, side projects, creative outlets. They nourish your soul.
- **Character** – Who you become matters more than what you earn.
- **Contribution** – How are you making someone's life better?

The Goal Is Wholeness, Not Just Achievement

You'll meet people who have "made it" but feel hollow inside.
And you'll meet others who may not be on magazine covers—but are content, fulfilled, and living with purpose.

Aim to be the latter.

A balanced, kind, growing, grateful human being.

So Yes—Build Your Career with Passion

Strive. Hustle. Aim high.

But also...

- Call your parents
- Take care of your body
- Spend time in nature
- Make time for people, not just deadlines
- Do things that light up your heart, not just your résumé

Because in the long run, your life won't be measured by promotions or paychecks.
It will be measured by the **love you gave, the growth you embraced, the difference you made, and the joy you felt.**

So build with intention.
Not just a career.
Build a life you're proud to live.

With perspective and purpose,
Ashish

A Final Letter: You Are The Author Of Your Story

Dear Friend,

You've made it to the final letter.
But really, this is just the beginning—of **your story.**

Through these pages, I've tried to share lessons, insights, and reminders that I hope will guide you. But no matter how much anyone writes or says—
the most important words in your life will be the ones you write... through your actions, your decisions, and your journey.

Because at the end of the day, **you are the author of your story.**

Not your parents.
Not your professors.
Not your peers.
Not society.

You.

Life Will Give You the Pages

Some will be exciting.
Some will be ordinary.
Some will be heartbreaking.
Some will be magical.

But you get to decide the theme.

You get to choose the response.
You get to define the plot twist.
You get to build the ending.

Don't Wait for Permission

Start where you are.
With what you have.
And who you are right now.

The world doesn't need you to be perfect.
It just needs you to show up with honesty, effort, and heart.

Write boldly.
Make mistakes.
Turn the page.
Keep going.

And When You Look Back One Day...

I hope you smile at how far you came.
At the dreams you chased, the risks you took, the growth you embraced, and the lives you touched.

Your story doesn't have to be loud to be legendary.
It just has to be **true to you.**

Thank you for letting me walk beside you for a few pages of your journey.
Now it's your turn.

Pick up the pen.
Write your story.

Live it well.

With all my belief in you,
Ashish

Your Career Blueprint – A 10-step Action Plan

Dear College Friend,

Reading is only the first step.
Action is where transformation happens.

Now that you've reflected on all the letters, it's time to build your own Career Blueprint—a 10-step action plan to take charge of your future, one move at a time.

Step 1: Discover Your Strength Zone

Take time to understand what you're good at and what excites you.

- List your top 3 skills and interests.
- Take personality/career assessments (like MBTI, StrengthsFinder, or Ikigai).

Step 2: Set a 1-Year Career Goal

Have a clear, short-term goal to give direction to your efforts.

- Example: "By this time next year, I want to land an internship in marketing."
- Make your goal specific, measurable, and time-bound.

Step 3: Build Real Skills

Pick 2–3 key skills aligned with your career goal and start learning.

- Join online courses, attend workshops, build projects.
- Track your progress weekly.

Step 4: Create a Powerful Resume & LinkedIn Profile

Start early, update often.

- Highlight internships, projects, achievements, and relevant skills.
- Ask mentors or seniors to review it for feedback.

Step 5: Do at Least 2 Internships Before Final Year

Don't wait. Internships give exposure, clarity, and connections.

- Target companies, startups, or NGOs in your field of interest.
- Apply proactively and follow up.

Step 6: Build a Personal Brand

Start putting your voice and value out in the world.

- Write content, share your learning, showcase your work online.

- Be active on platforms like LinkedIn, YouTube, or Medium.

Step 7: Find 1–2 Mentors

Reach out to seniors, alumni, or professionals you admire.

- Ask for advice, feedback, or short conversations.
- Stay connected and learn from their journey.

Step 8: Start a Side Project

Create something that reflects your passion and skills.

- A blog, app, Instagram page, newsletter, or research paper—anything!
- Document the process and results.

Step 9: Learn to Network Authentically

Start building your network before you need it.

- Attend events, reach out online, be genuinely curious.
- Keep a list of professional contacts and follow up periodically.

Step 10: Reflect & Realign Every 3 Months

Pause to ask:

- What did I do well?
- What needs improvement?
- What's my next step?

Career-building is not a straight line. Be flexible. Be focused.

Final Tip:

Consistency beats intensity.
You don't need to do everything in one day—just something every day.

This is your blueprint. Use it. Tweak it. Own it.

The future isn't something you wait for.
It's something you build—step by step.

With all my belief in your journey,
Ashish